CELLS, GENES, AND CHROMOSOMES

Text: Núria Roca and Marta Serrano
Illustrations: Antonio Muñoz Tenllado

La célula, el origen de la vida © Copyright Parramón
Ediciones, S.A., 1995 Published by
Parramón Ediciones, S.A., Barcelona, Spain.

Printed and bound in Spain.

Chelsea House Publishers
1974 Sproul Road, Suite 400
Broomall, PA 19008-0914

The Chelsea House world wide web address is
www.chelseahouse.com

Library of Congress Cataloging-in-Publication Data
Applied for

ISBN 0-7910-3154-3

Contents

INVISIBLE WORLD

CELLS, GENES, AND CHROMOSOMES

CHELSEA HOUSE PUBLISHERS

Philadelphia

The Origin of Life

The prehistoric world experienced a series of dramatic changes long before the existence of life was possible. The earth was formed approximately 4,600 million years ago, when the clouds of gas and dust particles that circled around the sun solidified. The primitive planet's atmosphere was composed of gases given off by its molten interior. When the earth's temperature dropped, one of these gases in the atmosphere, water vapor, fell to the ground as torrential rain and created the oceans. This liquid water is a very rare phenomenon in the solar system, and without it living organisms could not exist.

Alexander Ivanovich Oparin, a 20th-century Soviet biochemist, attempted to explain how life was created under these conditions. His theory states that the chemical components in the early atmosphere reacted spontaneously to form simple organic compounds. These organic molecules accumulated in the oceans over long periods of time, generating what Oparin called a nutritious or primordial soup. The molecules eventually combined to make linked molecules in the form of semiliquid droplets, with an internal space separated from the outside, called coacervations. With time some of these evolved into increasingly complex and stable forms, until they acquired the basic characteristic of a living thing, and the first cells appeared. Some of these cells joined together to form colonies that evolved into the first multicellular organisms, from which all living things descended.

Lightning and the high temperatures of the lava on the primitive earth provided the heat necessary for the atmosphere's chemical components to link and form simple compounds. Over millions of years these organic molecules combined until eventually they were converted into the precursors of proteins and nucleic acids, the building blocks of life.

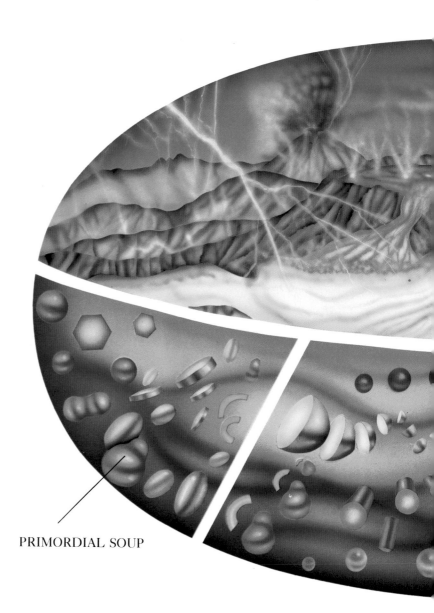

PRIMORDIAL SOUP

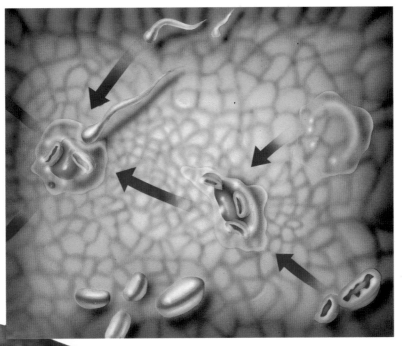

◀ *A cell absorbs two respiratory cells and links up with a mobile cell, forming a more complex cell equipped with organelles.*

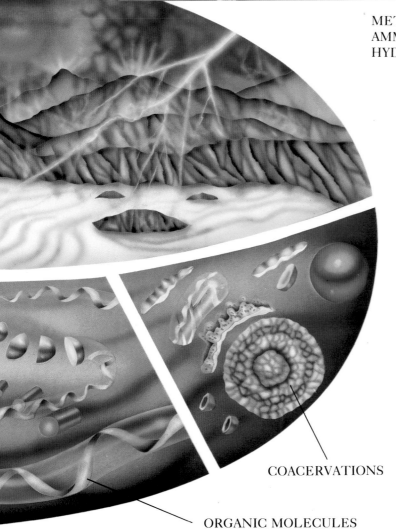

METHANE
AMMONIA
HYDROGEN

ELECTRODES

WATER
VAPOR

WATER

DEPOSIT
(AMINO ACIDS)

COACERVATIONS

ORGANIC MOLECULES

▲
In 1952, researcher Stanley Miller tried to reproduce the atmospheric conditions of the primitive earth by creating a mixture of methane, *ammonia, and water vapor. After exposing this mixture to various electric charges, he found that some of the organic compounds necessary for life had been formed.*

"Living" Molecules

Living organisms are composed of inorganic molecules such as water, which are not exclusive to living things, and organic molecules, which exist only in living things. Organic molecules—including carbohydrates, lipids, proteins, and nucleic acids—are primarily made of four elements: carbon, oxygen, hydrogen, and nitrogen.

Carbohydrates, or sugars, are a group of compounds formed from one or more basic units called monosaccharides. These units link together to form disaccharides or polysaccharides. Carbohydrates provide an important source of fuel for the cell. The body stores excess carbohydrates as either glycogen or fat.

Lipids, or fats, are a group of compounds that are not soluble in water. They compose part of the cell membrane. In addition, they are a main source of energy for cells, lasting over a longer period of time than carbohydrates.

Proteins are a type of organic compound consisting of a series of basic units called amino acids. The most abundant cellular compounds, proteins perform a key role in almost all biological processes: for example, some facilitate the chemical reactions that take place in a cell, while others fill a defensive role or transport substances.

Nucleic acids, made up of smaller units called nucleotides, are the most complex organic molecules. The different kinds of ribonucleic acid (RNA) make the synthesis of proteins possible. The other type of nucleic acid, deoxyribonucleic acid (DNA), transmits hereditary characteristics from one generation to the next.

Glycogen consists of a long chain of glucose molecules, a type of monosaccharide. Carbohydrates are stored as glycogen in animal tissues, and the chain is broken down to release glucose molecules as the body requires energy.

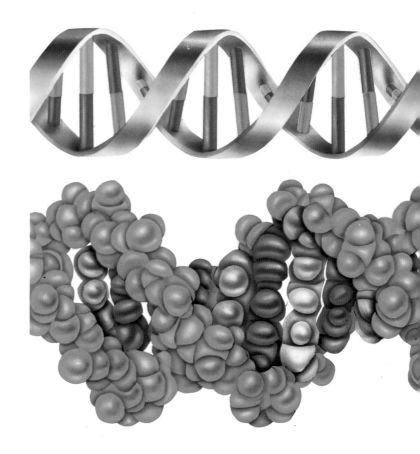

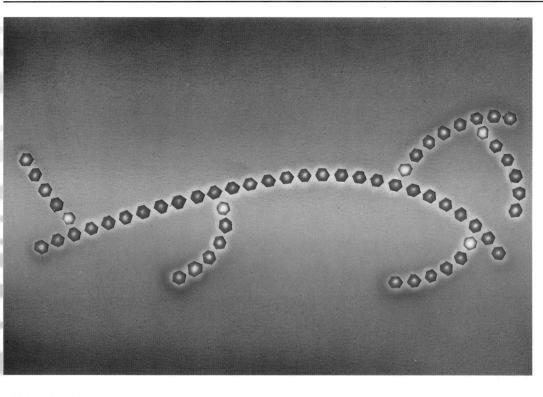

This picture is a representation of a DNA molecule, enlarged four million times.

▼

DNA MOLECULE

SIMPLIFIED VIEW

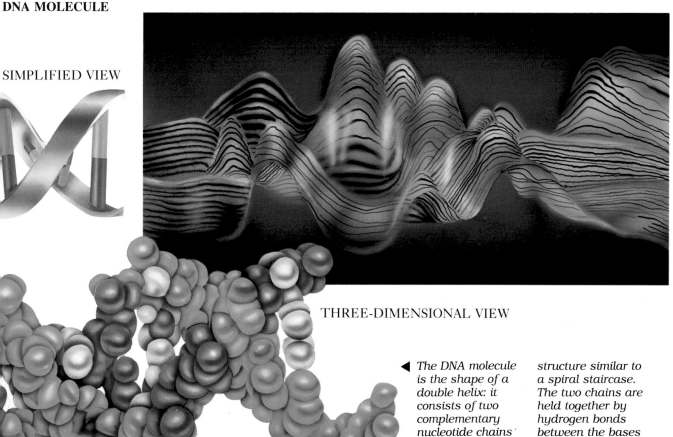

THREE-DIMENSIONAL VIEW

◄ *The DNA molecule is the shape of a double helix: it consists of two complementary nucleotide chains that are coiled in parallel to create a structure similar to a spiral staircase. The two chains are held together by hydrogen bonds between the bases of the nucleotides.*

Inside a Cell

All the cells in the human body, as well as the cells of most living organisms, share certain basic characteristics: the cell membrane or plasma membrane, the cytoplasm, and the nucleus.

The cell membrane wraps around the cell, containing the cytoplasm. Acting as a semipermeable barrier, the cell membrane regulates the passage of substances into and out of the cell.

The cytoplasm is a jellylike substance that often contains stored substances and structures called organelles that have specific functions. One main type of organelle, the lysosome, contains enzymes that digest particles such as bacteria. Ribosomes, globular particles that contain RNA, are responsible for synthesizing proteins. The ribosomes can move freely in the cytoplasm or can be located against the walls of the endoplasmic reticulum, a network of interconnected cavities. Besides being the site of protein and lipid production, the endoplasmic reticulum plays a role in transporting materials inside the cell. The Golgi apparatus, a collection of vesicles, stores and later secretes the compounds manufactured in the endoplasmic reticulum. Organelles called mitochondria engage in cellular respiration, which produces the energy needed for the cell to carry out all its functions.

The nucleus, which is separated from the cytoplasm by its own membrane, is the main organelle of the cell, necessary for the cell's growth and reproduction. The chromosomes in the nucleus are long threads of DNA composed of sequences of genes, each one of which contains information about cellular functions.

Cells are grouped ▶ *into two types: eukaryotic cells, found in humans and all other multicellular creatures, and prokaryotic cells, found in bacteria and other simple, unicellular organisms.*

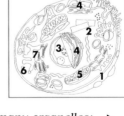

The three primary parts of an animal cell are: the cell membrane (1), the cytoplasm (2), and the nucleus (3). In addition, the cytoplasm holds *many organelles:* ▶ *the endoplasmic reticulum (4), the mitochondria (5), the lysosomes (6), and the Golgi apparatus (7).*

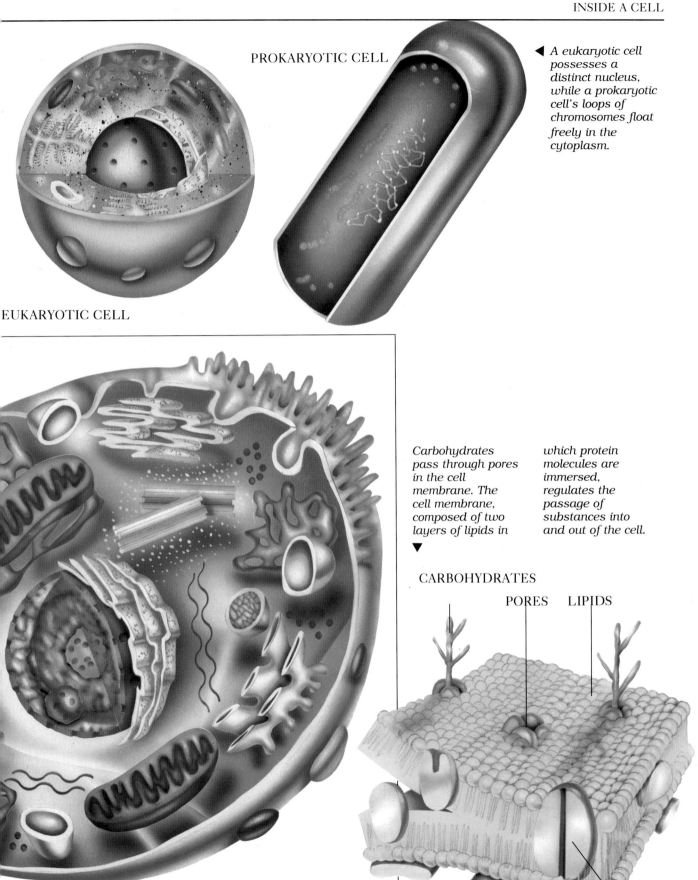

PROKARYOTIC CELL

◀ *A eukaryotic cell possesses a distinct nucleus, while a prokaryotic cell's loops of chromosomes float freely in the cytoplasm.*

EUKARYOTIC CELL

Carbohydrates pass through pores in the cell membrane. The cell membrane, composed of two layers of lipids in ▼ *which protein molecules are immersed, regulates the passage of substances into and out of the cell.*

CARBOHYDRATES

PORES   LIPIDS

PROTEINS

PROTEINS

The Nourishment of Cells

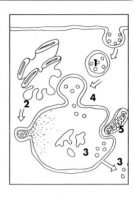

All cells, from the simplest to the most evolved, need fuel to carry out each one of their vital functions, as well as to maintain their structures and to create new ones. Through cellular nutrition, the cell takes in certain materials and unleashes the energy in them.

Cellular nutrition consists of different stages. First the cell has to ingest the necessary substances. Small substances pass through the cell membrane by diffusion without any difficulty but larger substances require more work. In a process called endocytosis, large particles or droplets of liquid are engulfed by part of the cell.

Phagocytes, which engulf solid particles, often surround and digest bacteria and other harmful substances.

After the necessary substances are incorporated into the cell, lysosomes release enzymes to digest them. These enzymes can also break down components of the cell that must be replaced, such as old organelles. The products of this digestion then pass into the cytoplasm and incorporate themselves into the cellular metabolism. Sometimes these products are used in the construction of complex molecules such as proteins and fats, called anabolism. Mitochondria also use these products in catabolism, breaking them down even further to release energy for the cell.

The vesicle (1) ingested into the cell by endocytosis is surrounded by lysosomes (2), organelles that release enzymes capable of digesting complex molecules and transforming them into simple molecules (3). This process is called heterophagy (4), as opposed to autophagy (5), where the cell's own structures, such as old organelles, are broken down.

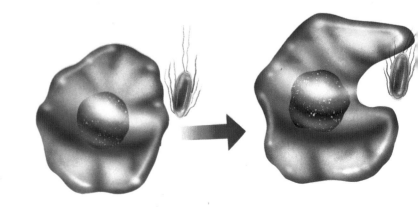

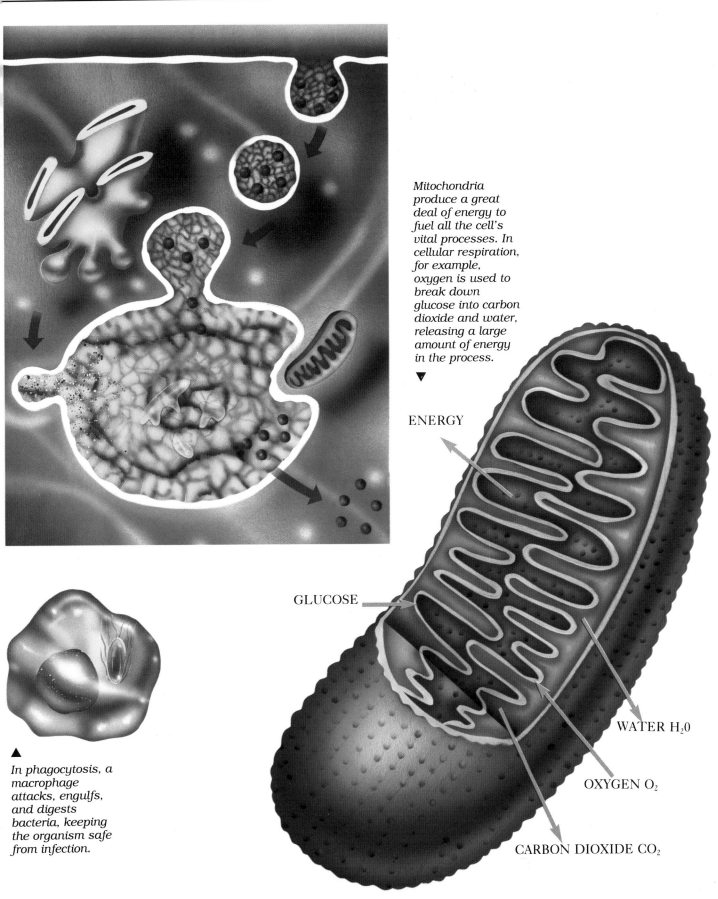

Mitochondria produce a great deal of energy to fuel all the cell's vital processes. In cellular respiration, for example, oxygen is used to break down glucose into carbon dioxide and water, releasing a large amount of energy in the process.
▼

ENERGY

GLUCOSE

WATER H_2O

OXYGEN O_2

CARBON DIOXIDE CO_2

▲
In phagocytosis, a macrophage attacks, engulfs, and digests bacteria, keeping the organism safe from infection.

Relating to the Outside Environment

Cells maintain close contact with their external environment in order to receive as much information as possible. They can detect specific changes occurring around them, quickly responding in a way that will best ensure their survival. The cell membrane is particularly sensitive in its role as a selective barrier against the passage of substances. This cellular sensitivity can be activated by a variety of stimuli, including chemical, physical, thermal, and electrical kinds.

Certain cells in the human body have a greater sensitivity to physical and chemical stimuli, such as cells in the skin that detect changes in temperature or those in the eye and ear that perceive light or sound. These receptor cells transform their information into electrical messages to the sensory nervous system.

Another common cellular response to various stimuli is movement of some kind. Some cells can extend their cytoplasm and cell membrane in the form of a false foot, or pseudopod, to move like an amoeba. When germs invade the body, scavenging cells called macrophages rush to the infected area to destroy the bacteria by phagocytosis.

Spermatozoa also possess great motility. By whipping around its tail, or flagella, the sperm cell gains a steady speed in its journey to fertilize the ovum.

Another example from the human body is the lining cells of the respiratory ducts, such as the nasal cavity. These cells have numerous tiny, hairlike extensions called cilia, which use a sweeping movement to help expel any foreign particles such as dust or bacteria that could harm the respiratory apparatus.

The cilia, found in some areas of the mucous membrane that lines the respiratory ducts, perform a waving motion to remove mucous and any foreign particles trapped in it.

▼

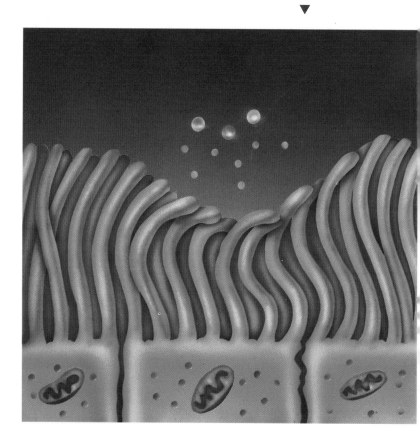

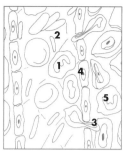

◀ When the body has an infection, leukocytes [1] are attracted to the problem area. They leave the bloodstream [2] by introducing pseudopods [3] between the endothelial cells [4] of the blood vessels and then move to destroy the invading microorganisms. Leukocytes that can move through the body are also called macrophages [5].

Driven by their thin, hairlike tail, spermatozoa generally move at a speed of one inch per minute on their way to the ovum.

▼

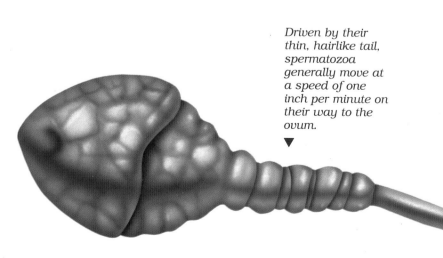

From a Zygote to an Adult

A key attribute of the cell is its ability to reproduce itself, creating simple new cells or whole new living beings. The cells in human beings multiply themselves in two different ways.

In meiosis, a cell division produces four daughter cells, each with 23 chromosomes, half the number of the original. This process only occurs in the reproductive organs, with the ovaries creating ova and the testicles manufacturing spermatozoa. When the ovum and spermatozoon unite, the resulting zygote has the usual 46 chromosomes, with half its genetic material coming from the mother and half from the father.

All the cells in our bodies come from one single cell, the zygote, which reproduces itself through mitosis. In mitosis, a single parent cell duplicates its genetic material and then divides to produce two daughter cells with identical chromosomes. Mitotic activity is especially intense during the embryonic stage, when the fetus is growing and developing in the mother's womb. The number of neurons formed by the time of birth never increases, but other body cells, such as those in the skin, are continually replaced through mitosis.

Mitosis allows a cell to divide and create two exact copies of itself.

▼

MITOSIS

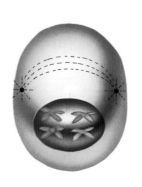  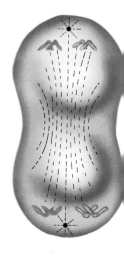

1. PROPHASE 2. METAPHASE 3. ANAPHASE

SPERMATOGENESIS

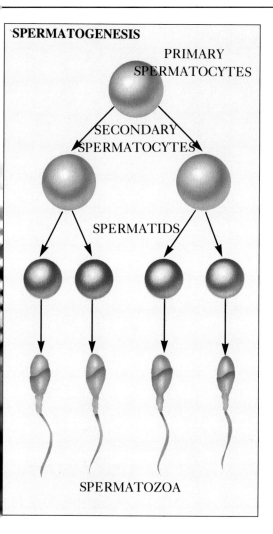

PRIMARY SPERMATOCYTES

SECONDARY SPERMATOCYTES

SPERMATIDS

SPERMATOZOA

OOGENESIS

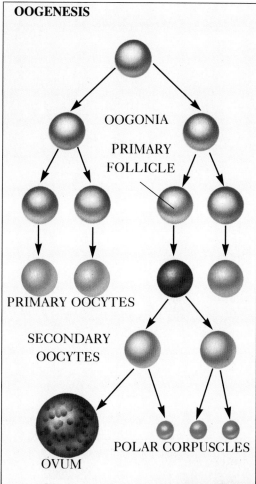

OOGONIA

PRIMARY FOLLICLE

PRIMARY OOCYTES

SECONDARY OOCYTES

OVUM

POLAR CORPUSCLES

◀ *Meiosis is the type of cell division that produces sexual cells. The illustration shows the different phases that take place in spermatogenesis, the formation of spermatozoa, and in oogenesis, the formation of ova. In addition to the ovum formed during oogenesis, polar corpuscles that are not involved in fertilization are also produced.*

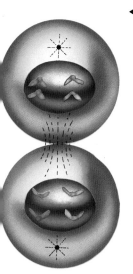

◀ *There are four stages in mitosis: the prophase, in which the nuclear membrane dissolves; the metaphase, in which the chromosomes situate themselves in the center of the cell; the anaphase, in which the chromatids of each chromosome separate toward opposite extremes of the cell; and the telophase, in which the cell divides in two.*

4. TELOPHASE

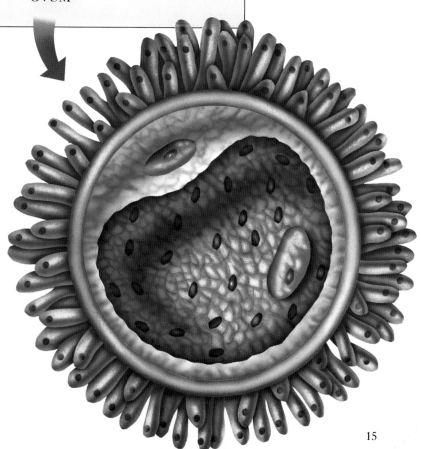

Different Forms, Different Functions

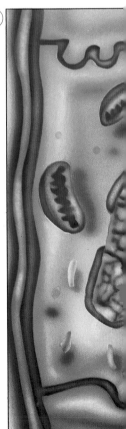

Although all the body's cells originate from the zygote and possess identical genetic material, not all of them have the same shape, structure, and size. In multicellular organisms, it is more efficient for cells to specialize and divide the work, rather than having each cell carry out all the vital activities. Specialization causes cells to accentuate the structures best suited to certain processes, while their ability to undergo other processes diminishes. Mechanisms develop so that only the genetic material that is expressed in a specialized cell contains information for its specific function.

The first mitotic divisions that the zygote undergoes create a group of cells that are identical. However, at a certain moment in the development of the embryo, the divisions begin to form different cellular lines, which will form different tissues. A tissue is a group of specialized cells that perform the same function, and so have morphological features in common. The tissue types include nerve tissue, muscular tissue, and bone tissue.

Tissue is combined to form organs such as the heart, the lungs, and the liver. Finally, several organs can unite to give rise to a system or an apparatus, which performs a more general function in the organism. For instance, the respiratory apparatus, whose task is to take in oxygen, is formed of a group of organs (nose, pharynx, larynx, trachea, bronchi, and lungs), which in turn are composed of different types of tissue (epithelial, cartilaginous, connective.)

All the cells in the human body have identical genetic material in their nuclei. However, the illustrations at right demonstrate how vastly different the structure of specialized cells can be. For example, the epithelial tissue that covers the stomach (1) has a prismatic form, numerous microvilli, and many mucus-secreting granules that produce a substance to protect the gastric cells from their own gastric acid. In contrast, the fibroblasts of connective tissue (2) are star-shaped and have a great number of ribosomes to synthesize proteins for collagen and elastic fibers. ▶

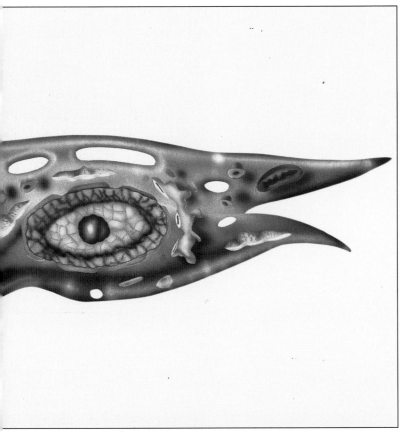

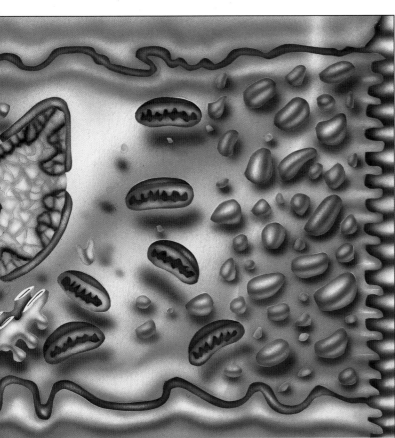

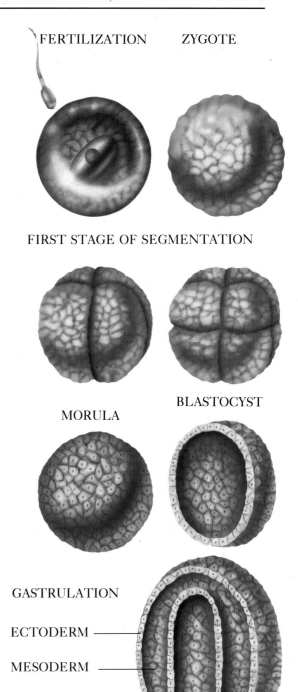

FERTILIZATION   ZYGOTE

FIRST STAGE OF SEGMENTATION

MORULA

BLASTOCYST

GASTRULATION

ECTODERM

MESODERM

ENDODERM

▲

Shown above is an
illustration of the
initial stages in the
development of an
embryo, which
begins with the
formation of a
zygote. It is after
the phase of
gastrulation, in
which three layers
of cells are formed,
that the cells begin
to differentiate.
Each one of these
layers will give
rise to different
types of tissue.

Supportive Tissues

The cells that support the human body together form three types of tissue: connective, cartilaginous, and bony tissue. Connective tissue, composed of a ground substance that contains fibers and other cells, supports or binds different organs in the body. The main cells of connective tissue are fibroblasts, which produce both the ground substance and fibers such as collagen. Connective tissue can also hold macrophages and fat cells. In the connective tissue of the skin's dermis, a dark-brown pigment called melanin can accumulate, giving the skin a tanned color.

Cartilage is a strong, elastic connective tissue made of fibers and cells called chondrocytes. Babies have much cartilage, but it appears in adults mainly in the nose, earlobes, epiglottis, and between the bones in joints.

Bone is the hard, dense tissue that forms the body's skeleton and stores calcium and manufactures some blood cells. Osteoblast cells create osteocytes, the mature bone cells, and osteoclast cells break down bone when necessary. Bones—together with cartilage and connective tissue—give the body its shape, support and protect the internal organs, and make movement possible.

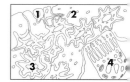

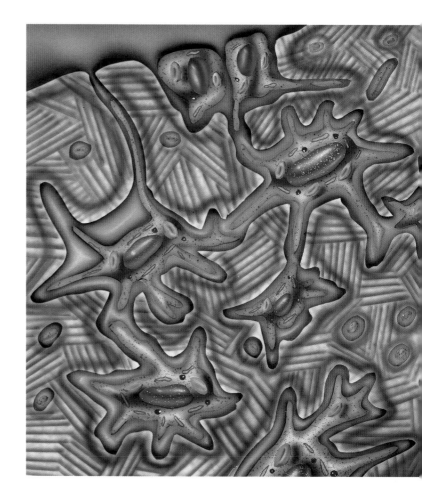

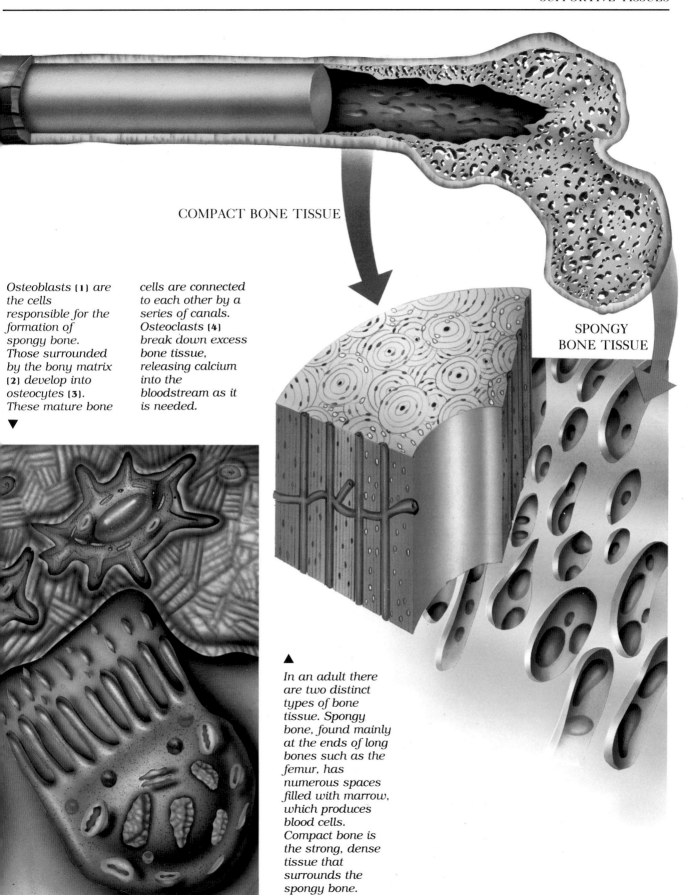

COMPACT BONE TISSUE

Osteoblasts [1] are the cells responsible for the formation of spongy bone. Those surrounded by the bony matrix [2] develop into osteocytes [3]. These mature bone ▼

cells are connected to each other by a series of canals. Osteoclasts [4] break down excess bone tissue, releasing calcium into the bloodstream as it is needed.

SPONGY BONE TISSUE

▲

In an adult there are two distinct types of bone tissue. Spongy bone, found mainly at the ends of long bones such as the femur, has numerous spaces filled with marrow, which produces blood cells. Compact bone is the strong, dense tissue that surrounds the spongy bone.

The Body's Covering

Certain tissues specialize in covering the body's surface, either internal or external. The cells in this epithelial tissue are closely linked together, without any fibrous material in between, and are separated from connective tissue underneath by a basement membrane.

Epithelium covers and protects the external surface of the body and lines its internal cavities. It can consist of either a single layer of cells or several layers. The epithelial cells on the outer layer of skin are flat and scalelike, while other types are shaped like columns. The upper respiratory tract is lined with columnar epithelial cells that have cilia, and the intestines contain epithelial cells with villi. Endothelium, made up of a single layer of flat cells, lines the inside of the heart, the blood vessels, and lymphatic vessels.

Some epithelial cells are able to secrete certain necessary substances. For example, these secretions can be for protection (gastric mucus), digestion (enzymes of the salivary glands), or for regulating other functions (perspiration). A gland is a group of cells or an organ that synthesizes and secretes particular substances. Exocrine glands have ducts to carry their secretions to specific places, such as a sweat gland with a duct to a pore in the skin. Endocrine glands secrete their products, such as hormones, directly into the bloodstream.

▶

The skin is composed of two main layers: the epidermis, made of epithelial tissue, and the dermis, made of connective tissue. The bottom layer under the dermis is mainly fatty tissue. The epidermis plays an important protective role for the body and works with certain glands in excreting substances. The illustration shows a sweat gland (1), a hair follicle (2), and sebaceous glands (3).

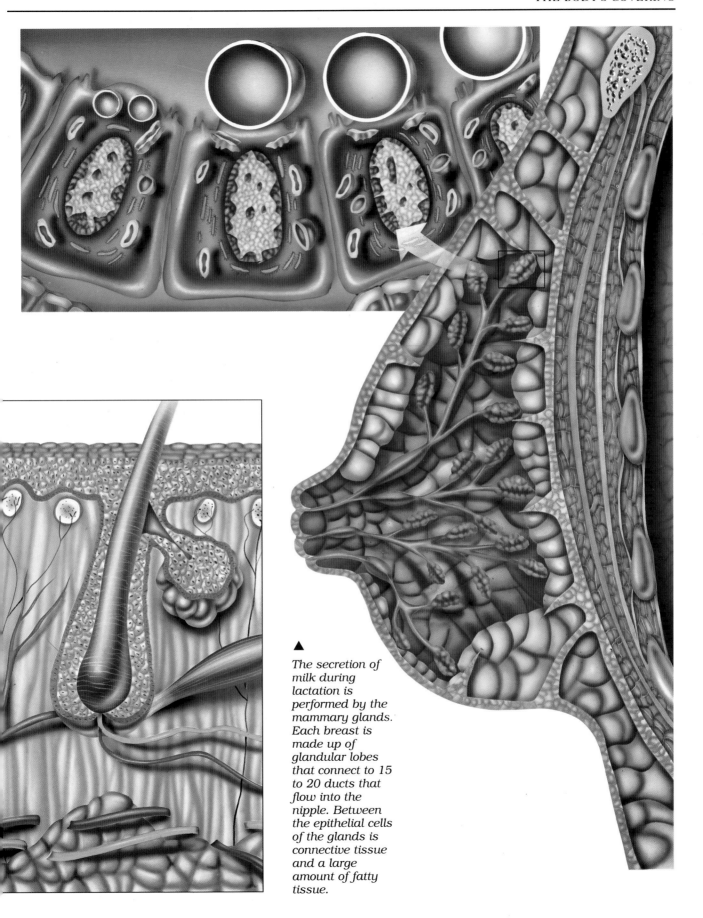

▲
The secretion of milk during lactation is performed by the mammary glands. Each breast is made up of glandular lobes that connect to 15 to 20 ducts that flow into the nipple. Between the epithelial cells of the glands is connective tissue and a large amount of fatty tissue.

Information Gatherers and Messengers

The nervous system receives and interprets stimuli, then sends messages to the appropriate organs to carry out a suitable response. This vital system is composed of two parts: neurons, highly specialized cells that conduct nerve impulses over long distances at high speed, and neuroglia, which provide protection and nutrition for the nerve cells.

Neurons possess a highly developed communication mechanism. Dendrites, short branches from the cell body, receive messages from other neurons and transmit the information as electrical signals to the neuron's cell body and axon. Then the axon, which extends from the cell body in a single long branch that can reach up to several feet in length, carries the message to other cells. Since nerve cells are separated by gaps called synapses, the axon must transform the electrical impulse running down it into a chemical neurotransmitter, which crosses the gap and activates the dendrites of the next neuron.

The cytoplasm of the neuron contains all the organelles of a normal cell, although the endoplasmic reticulum is more highly developed and there are many ribosomes, due to the large amount of protein synthesis that takes place in the neuron. The nerve cell in humans is also unusual because it no longer reproduces itself after birth.

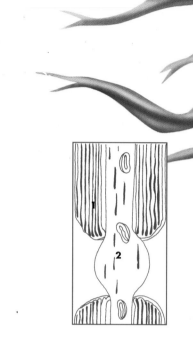

CROSS-SECTION
OF AN AXON

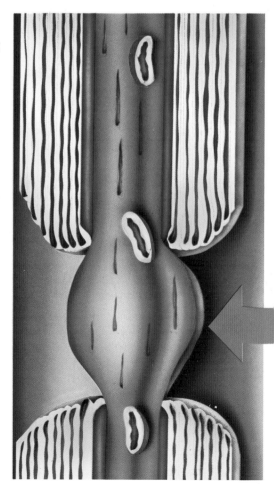

Some axons are covered by a fatty substance called myelin (1) that insulates the axon, increasing the efficiency and speed of the transmission; the thickest nerve fibers can transmit impulses at a speed of roughly 200 miles per hour. There are periodic gaps, called Ranvier's nodes (2), in the myelin sheath where the axon is surrounded only by Schwann cells, which manufacture myelin.

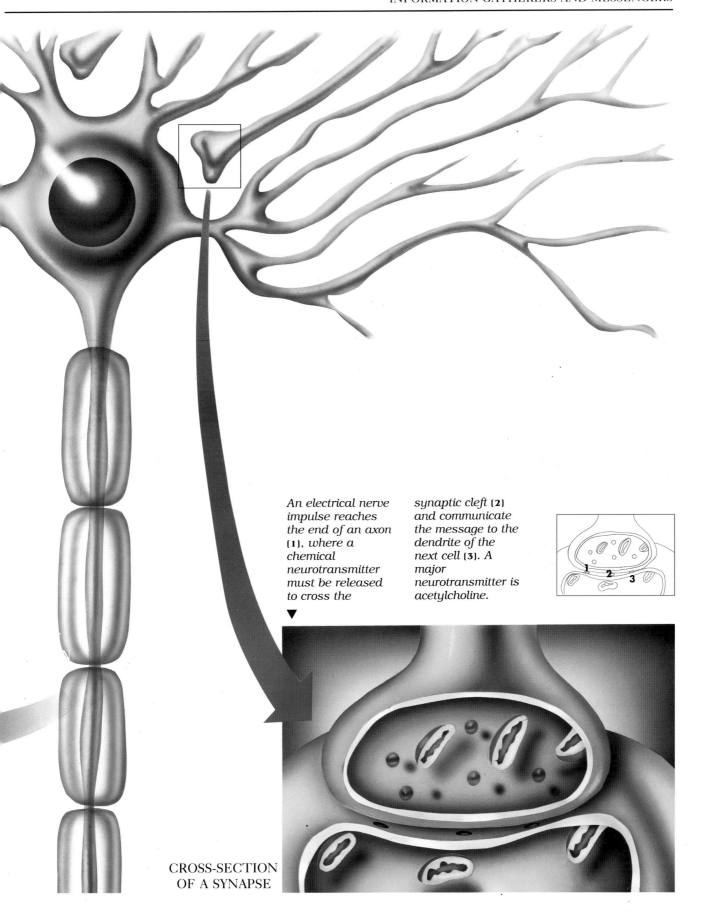

An electrical nerve impulse reaches the end of an axon [1], where a chemical neurotransmitter must be released to cross the synaptic cleft [2] and communicate the message to the dendrite of the next cell [3]. A major neurotransmitter is acetylcholine.

CROSS-SECTION OF A SYNAPSE

The Cells Behind Movement

The cells in muscle fiber, called myocytes, are specialized to perform contractions and relaxations that create movement or force. These cells possess two key proteins, actin and myosin, in their cytoplasm. Filaments of these proteins are grouped into myofibrils, which are then grouped into larger bundles called sarcomeres. In skeletal muscle cells, which also have several nuclei, the actin and myosin filaments are interspersed in light and dark bands.

Muscular contraction occurs when motor neurons transmit an instruction to the myocytes; humans can move skeletal muscles voluntarily, but smooth muscles, such as those in the digestive system, perform automatically and involuntarily. Once a motion command is received from the nervous system, the myofibrils of actin and myosin in the muscle cells slide over each other, shortening the length of the sarcomeres and thus causing the muscle to contract.

Because this process requires a large amount of energy, muscle cells have numerous mitochondria. Another particularity of muscle tissue is the high metabolism of calcium, which is necessary for contraction. In addition, myocytes possess myoglobin, a pigment that stores oxygen and gives muscles their characteristic red color.

There are different types of muscular tissue: skeletal muscle (1), whose function is locomotion, consists of striated fiber; the cardiac muscle (2), which causes the heart to beat, is made of a slightly different striated fiber; and smooth muscle (3), in which actin and myosin do not form bands, appears in blood vessels and the internal organs.

▼

1. SKELETAL MUSCLE
(STRIATED FIBER)

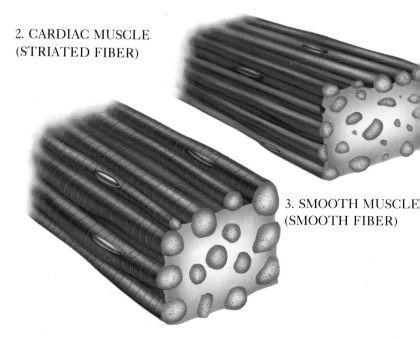

2. CARDIAC MUSCLE
(STRIATED FIBER)

3. SMOOTH MUSCLE
(SMOOTH FIBER)

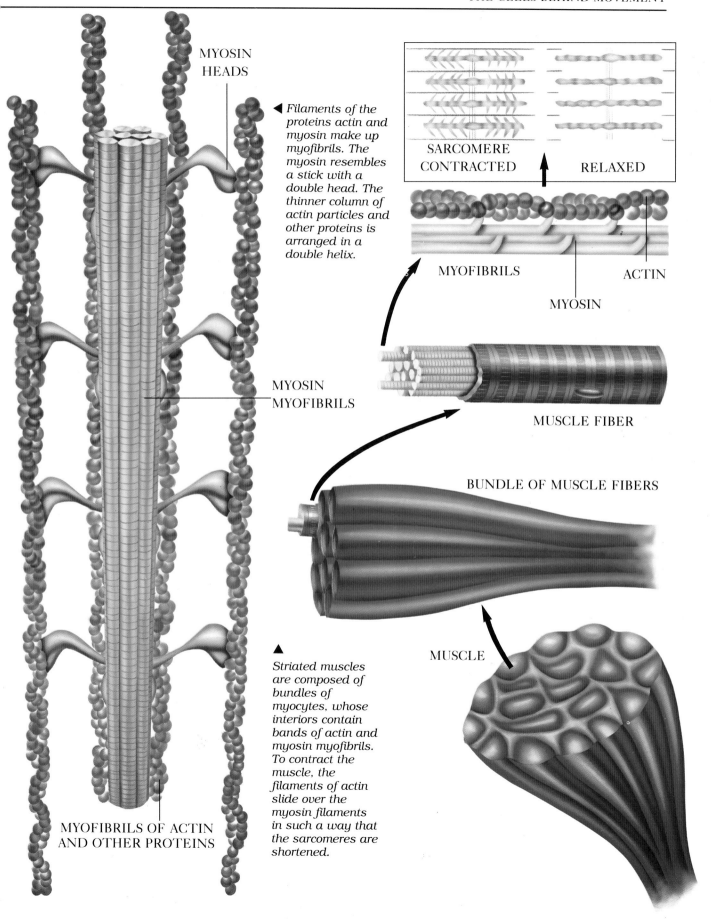

MYOSIN
HEADS

◀ *Filaments of the proteins actin and myosin make up myofibrils. The myosin resembles a stick with a double head. The thinner column of actin particles and other proteins is arranged in a double helix.*

SARCOMERE
CONTRACTED

RELAXED

MYOFIBRILS

MYOSIN

ACTIN

MYOSIN
MYOFIBRILS

MUSCLE FIBER

BUNDLE OF MUSCLE FIBERS

▲
Striated muscles are composed of bundles of myocytes, whose interiors contain bands of actin and myosin myofibrils. To contract the muscle, the filaments of actin slide over the myosin filaments in such a way that the sarcomeres are shortened.

MUSCLE

MYOFIBRILS OF ACTIN
AND OTHER PROTEINS

A Transportation System

In unicellular living things, nutrients move from one part of the organism to another without problem, by a process of diffusion. However, multicellular organisms as complex as humans require a whole transportation system to reach all their cells. Blood, a liquid that carries many different substances as it is pumped around the body through blood vessels, is the fundamental element of this system.

One of blood's most crucial tasks is the transportation of oxygen to all the body's cells. Suspended in the plasma (the liquid part of blood) are red blood cells called erythrocytes. These contain the protein hemoglobin, which carries and releases oxygen easily. The erythrocyte lacks a nucleus and has membranes flexible enough to squeeze through tiny capillaries. The most numerous component of blood, red blood cells live for nearly four months and are constantly replaced by new ones made in the bone marrow.

The blood also carries white blood cells, or leukocytes, which defend the body from infection. Besides having a nucleus, they are larger and less numerous than the erythrocytes. Some leukocytes produce antibodies, defense proteins that attach themselves to foreign particles. Others, such as neutrophils and monocytes, ingest and destroy germs.

Besides transporting substances such as blood cells, nutrients, and hormones, the blood helps to maintain the liquid balance in the body and to regulate the body's temperature. Blood cells called platelets produce clots when it is necessary to stop blood from flowing from a wound.

The three most important blood cells immersed in the liquid plasma are: white blood cells, which fight infection; red blood cells, which transport oxygen; and platelets, which coagulate the blood. ▶

There are many varieties of leukocytes, which are manufactured in the bone marrow. Three basic cellular types are myeloblasts, lymphoblasts, and monoblasts, which can leave the blood vessels and transform themselves into macrophages.

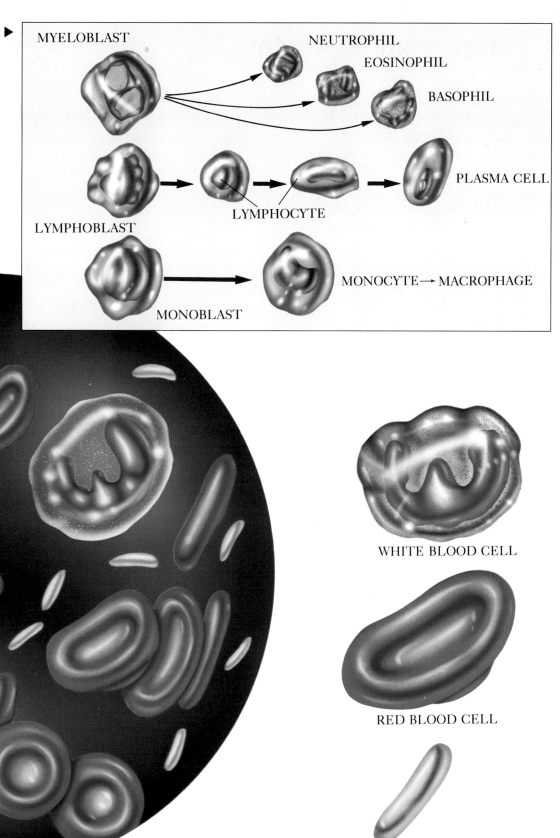

MYELOBLAST

NEUTROPHIL

EOSINOPHIL

BASOPHIL

PLASMA CELL

LYMPHOCYTE

LYMPHOBLAST

MONOCYTE → MACROPHAGE

MONOBLAST

WHITE BLOOD CELL

RED BLOOD CELL

PLATELET

Observing and Understanding

Viewing Cells

Because of their extraordinarily small size, cells are impossible to see without using a microscope. To view a sample of cells clearly under a microscope, it should be spread out on a glass slide, stained with a suitable dye, and illuminated correctly. Using a microscope is very simple: it only takes a little practice to learn how prepare a sample and focus the lens.

A microscope allows you to explore the smallest units of living organisms. Some cells may need to be stained before they become visible.
▼

Seeing Your Own Cells

If you want to examine your own cells, you can carry out the following experiment. You will need a slide, a slide cover, and some blue methylene. With a clean, small spatula, gently scrape along the inside of your cheek. Then spread the whitish liquid in a very thin film on the slide. Wait for it to dry, and then put a small amount of blue methylene on the slide. After

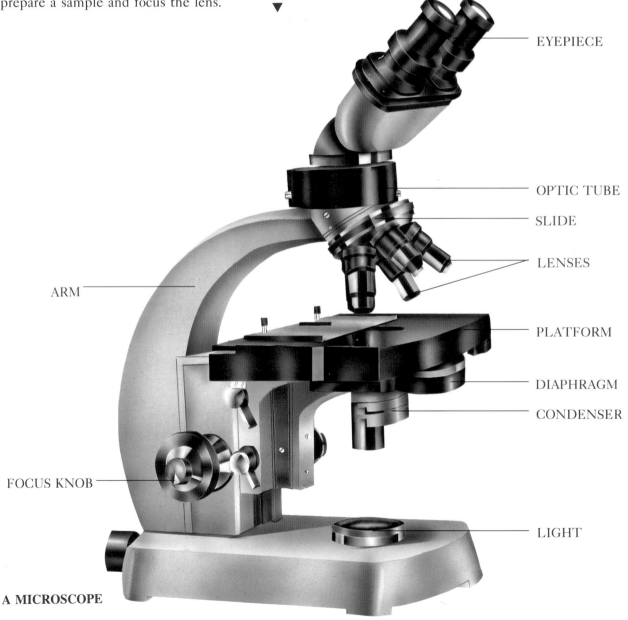

EYEPIECE

OPTIC TUBE

SLIDE

LENSES

ARM

PLATFORM

DIAPHRAGM

CONDENSER

FOCUS KNOB

LIGHT

A MICROSCOPE

three or four minutes, rinse off the blue colorant with some water. Next put on the slide cover and place the slide on the microscope platform.

You should be able to observe some cells with outlined edges, their nuclei, and around them a series of spots, which are the organelles of the cellular cytoplasm. These are epithelial cells from the lining of the buccal cavity.

Epithelial cells from the buccal cavity are easily observed if you carefully spread the white liquid you have obtained so that the cells will not be piled on top of each other. To spread it you can pass the edge of another slide over the preparation.

▼

Your Blood Under the Microscope

If you want to see your blood cells, first carefully clean and disinfect (with rubbing alcohol) your fingertip. Make a tiny prick with a sterilized needle to get a small amount of blood. If you do this experiment with someone else, make sure that you do not under any circumstances use the same needle. Next, gently squeeze a drop of blood onto a slide and spread it out well. Place the slide cover on top of it and finally put it under the microscope. You will only be able to see the red blood cells, because a special stain is required for the white ones. Finally, remember to once again wash and disinfect your finger to prevent infection.

*When you are ready to prick your finger, you must take special care to avoid possible infection. Clean and disinfect the finger well and obtain a sterile needle. **Never use a needle that has already been used**.*

▼

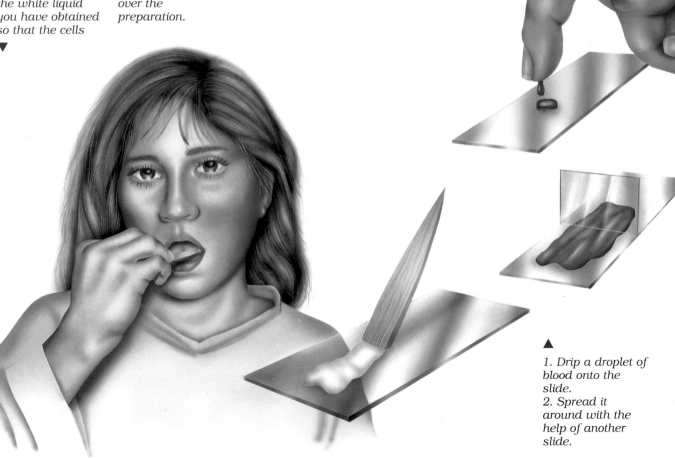

▲
*1. Drip a droplet of blood onto the slide.
2. Spread it around with the help of another slide.*

Glossary

deoxyribonucleic acid (DNA) *a double-helix structure of nucleotides that contains all of a cell's genetic information and controls its heredity*

diffusion *the movement of molecules or ions from areas where they are abundant to others where they are not*

epithelium *the tissue that covers the external surface of the body and lines its internal cavities*

macrophage *a scavenging cell that travels through the body to fight bacteria and other foreign particles*

meiosis *a type of cell division, occurring only in the formation of ova and sperm, that produces daughter cells with only half the number of chromosomes of the original*

metabolism *a combination of physical and chemical processes by which the material of the body is built and maintained (anabolism) and the energy the organism needs is produced (catabolism)*

mitochondria *the organelles that produce energy for the cell*

mitosis *a process by which a cell produces two daughter cells identical to itself*

nerve impulse *an electrical signal sent from neuron to neuron*

nucleus *a structure within a cell that contains its genetic material and is essential to all its functions*

organic compounds *substances that only exist in living things and are composed mainly of carbon, hydrogen, oxygen and nitrogen*

ribonucleic acid (RNA) *a nucleic acid found in the cell's nucleus and cytoplasm that synthesizes proteins*

stimulus *any change in the environment that acts on an organism or a cell and causes it to react*

vesicles *small sacks, containing various substances, that are surrounded by a membrane and are found in cytoplasm*

zygote *a fertilized ovum before cell division begins*

Index